We Snap in Silence

We Snap in Silence

Unveiling Private Pain and Finding Perfect
Peace as a Woman, Wife, and Mother

by

LaVender S. Williams

Contents

Acknowledgments

I must publicly express my thanks to those who assisted in the completion of this long awaited for publication.

To the many women who expressed a need for this book: your openness encouraged me and will help others embrace peace. Elizabeth Costales, the best editor, for capturing the essence of my words and turning it into a published project; don't leave me. Johnny L. Shedrick, my father, for pushing me to be the best in everything; your passionate love for books planted seeds for this first work. You're my best critic. Rosie L. Shedrick, my mother: thank you for showing me what peace was before I knew it for myself. There is no other like my mother. My sister, Lavern, who assists and collaborates in everything I do. My sister Deborah, for patiently designing the book cover to my satisfaction. Shirley Harris, my sister in Christ, for "my gift from God" and confirming the timing to publish. Yvonne B. Scott, my prayer partner, for your continual prayers and tireless encouragement. Javan and Jaylan, my sons, for taking me to my limit and loving me even when I *snapped*. Without you, this book would not be. Kevin L. Williams, my husband and friend for allowing me to expose our marriage within these pages. Thank you for putting up with me and loving me until I found peace in my life as a woman, wife, and mother. Thank you for supporting me in yet another project. I love you!

Introduction

If you have never had a bad day, this book may not be for you. If you have it all together as a woman, are completely satisfied in your marriage, and have children that never ruffle your feathers, I encourage you to pass this book on to a friend. On the other hand, if you desire to experience fulfillment as a woman, wife, and mother while maintaining your peace of mind, continue reading!

This book begins by revealing a secret women share and as senseless as it sounds, we attempt to hide this secret from one another. We may never publicly admit it, but there are days we feel little value and worth in ourselves. As mothers, there are days we feel we are about to lose our minds. As wives, we share days of feeling unloved and sometimes used. We go to work everyday, whether in the home or outside the home, as if everything in our life is okay. We care for our children hoping they won't see the pain we mask. Some of us go to church Sunday after Sunday, silently suffering in the pews. To put it plainly, we play the game of charades. The object of the game of charades is to find the appropriate game face for your particular situation and wear it to the best of your ability. Not only does playing the game welcome unnecessary stress in our life, but the pressure to play may cause us to snap…in silence.

Women are hurting, *always* tired, and often stressed out as wives and mothers. We burn the candle at both ends, yet rarely speak of it. When we are together, we laugh and swap comical stories about our children and life in general. We say very little about our husbands and go home feeling good about how well we played the game. Being a woman is a high-pressure job, and I can't think of one high-pressure job that isn't accompanied by stress--the roles of wife and mother are no exception. Mothers have been overlooked long enough; wives can hardly help themselves but are called to be helpmates. This book not only exposes our shared secret, but also will help our families, friends, and mothers-to-be recognize the challenges endured on the journey of womanhood and teach them how to help us avoid snapping in silence.

I Am Who I Am

I've realized the importance of meeting myself where I am. My personality, demeanor, moods, and weird idiosyncrasies make up my total being. Accepting myself (whether I like me or not) has made living my life easier. Trying to portray the always-happy woman with the flawless children and always-lovable husband is not my calling. I am called to be transparent enough to show women they are not alone on this journey. Trying to measure up to another woman is way too much work. We are all wired differently. We are a direct result of a combination of our genes, childhood, and environment. Mix those components with our ability to make choices and... ta-da!

Finally in my forties I can freely say, "I am who I am." I looked in the mirror one day and said, "Where have you been all my life?" I would love to have my deceased grandmother's strength, my mother's patience, and my mentor's wisdom, yet I have me, therefore, me is what you get. I've turned my charades game card in. The mask I wore for years has been put to rest; it began to suffocate me as my true being began to unveil. I'm a stronger woman, more supportive wife, and more attentive mother as I allow me to be me. I have a newfound freedom in life as I live within my self-recognized strengths, weaknesses, and imperfections. I am what I am.

There are countless books illustrating the roles of wife and mother and just as many others communicating the spirit of a woman. Although I've read my share, none has captured my attention in regards to the reality of the three demanding roles. The reality not only includes the apparent highs and the lows, but it also engages the exigent situations and days, which sometimes causes us to snap in silence. Hearing at least one more woman admit she occasionally struggles in her roles would be a consolation. Reading another's search for her peace of mind in the midst of chaos would make me feel normal.

Is there peace to be found? Yes, by the grace of God while going through my own mess, I figured it out. I have found the recipe to keeping my peace of mind as a woman, wife, and mother. I have personally tested and tried the recipe over and over and if followed correctly, it works without fail. Within these pages is your personal copy of the recipe.

By sharing my own highs and lows, my hope is that there will be something here for every woman. I pray each reader will recognize the gift of perfect peace as we live our lives with the continual battles we encounter.

We Have the Power

Because of our vast diversity, women hold a unique force to empower and influence the world one home at a time. Admitting our shared secret and lovingly accepting one another will allow us to come together regardless of our race, creed, or family status. One by one, we can begin turning our charades game cards in as we recognize our value and significance as women, wives, and mothers. Unfortunately, instead of allowing the diversity to sustain our bond, it disconnects. What a powerful web we can weave by accepting and encouraging each other instead of judging and condemning. It would be wonderful if we could give the gift of acceptance to each other on Mother's Day instead of looking for once a year accolades and flowers from others.

One weekend I met a mother of six children who had never been married. After sharing this information, she immediately asked me not to hold it against her because so many women do. My reaction to this mother could have encouraged her or broken her spirit. We all have made mistakes at different degrees. Acceptance is critical in womanhood, yet we fall short.

I have a dear friend, Sandy, who is an Atheist. Sandy and I don't allow our beliefs to interfere with our camaraderie as women and our shared path of motherhood. Actually, our differences have strengthened our relationship. Sandy was very hesitant of sharing her views with me. She was a Christian when we met. There was no acceptable reaction to Sandy except to love and accept her just the same, if not more. Our bond is womanhood, not our beliefs. Sandy and I have different views on raising our children, homeschooling, religion, God, and other major issues. Our differences have taught me the importance of meeting others where they are. It has also taught me to love myself enough to freely be me--regardless of what others think or expect from me.

Women. We are different, yet we have one pivotal foundation. We were created with uniqueness and purpose. Allowing our diversity to disturb our natural harmony forfeits our power to make a difference; we deny the world of change. This book is not intended to persuade you to make different choices in your style of mothering or challenge how you support your husband. My intentions are to invite you to join me on the pathway to perfect peace as a woman, wife, and mother. Are you open to allowing optimistic change to begin? Are you open to allowing optimistic change to begin *in you*?

What's Behind the Makeup?

I come in contact with countless women, married and single, who feel they are alone in their feelings of dissatisfaction and inadequacy. For various reasons, women are not comfortable revealing these emotions openly, so it's kept a secret. Because it's a secret, our true self is masked. We hide behind makeup with a perfectly painted smile. We have mastered the game of charades. We build walls around our emotions by isolating ourselves from others, pouring into our jobs or school, working out, and sometimes we fill our plates with church ministry and volunteer work. Our goals and dreams are also used to camouflage our emotions. Of course we don't feel this way all the time, but each of us has experienced these feelings at some point in our life.

Is it necessary to disclose our true feelings of being burned out? Is it necessary to share our matrimony mess? Is it okay to say we need a break from our children? Why not? We all occasionally share these feelings, so why not share? What's the secret? Well, we're supposed to have it all together! We're labeled a "bad mother" if we reveal we are stressed out by our children. We're not a happy wife if we admit we don't want sex every night. God forbid we admit being dissatisfied with life--we'll be pointed at, talked about, preached to, and prayed over. Everyone will try to fix us! So then, we awaken day after day and pack on the makeup. The perfect smile is painted on, and when asked how we're doing, we say, "I'm fine!" Hell may be breaking loose in our home, yet we are "fine." Shhhh…it's a secret!

Silently Suffering

I've been a prime example of playing the game of charades. There was a season in my marriage when my husband and I didn't think we would live to see "happily ever after." We were either speaking of separating or not speaking at all. Through the entire sad season, I made sure I had my game face on and carried on as usual in public. When asked how I was doing, of course my reply was a happy, "Fine!" Being a churchgoer, I was the one sitting on the pews, silently suffering, wishing someone would allow me to pour my pain on them. I hoped someone would at least read my emotions and rescue me.

Why did I have to endure this alone? Why did everyone else seem so happy? Were they truly happy or were they in the game of charades with me? With everyone being so masked, it's hard to tell.

Once again, because we have been taught to go through our storms with strength and not speak of our hurt, no one knows what we go through. We are held in bondage by our own emotions and imitation strength. All I needed was one who would listen and not condemn me--just listen. As it turned out, the right woman crossed my path and allowed me to openly share my pain. She didn't try to fix the problem; she listened and encouraged me. Because this woman received me in love in spite of my mess, I am now able to remain unmasked in regards to my marriage while I share my pain and victory.

To this day, I am quick to correct anyone who thinks my marriage appears perfect. Perfect it is not, tested and tried it is. Unmasking began my healing process and placed me in a position to encourage other women. Prayerfully, my hope is that others will feel the liberty to unmask and begin their healing process also.

It's Not About You

As women, we are expected to be strong. We are taught to endure. We are programmed to walk through our pain. This may be true, but we forget or choose not to accept one important fact: our pain is not about us. Our pain is our *power* when shared. Playing charades only ruptures our potent bond as women. Our pain is another woman's gain. There is strength in our suffering as we carry the load of responsibilities of being a woman, wife, and mother.

By all means, walk through your pain! Endure! Just remember, if we don't share *how* we endured, we deny another woman the opportunity to know peace in her life--to be free. Because we are hesitant to share, we silently live in pain and frustration, which may cause us to snap in silence. We damage our health, our homes, our relationships, and our fellow women's hope--all because we play the popular game of charades.

We meet the world each day with our favorite game face. We are very careful to cover our true self. Sure, the outside looks great, yet our eyes speak words of fatigue, dissatisfaction, and hurt. One would never know of our long days and nights or the many challenges faced on a daily basis. We wear the masks of Able Anna, Bubbly Bernice, Cool Cathy, Dependable Donna, Energetic Eunice, Faithful Felicia, Gorgeous Gertrude, Happy Helen, Independent Irene, Joyful Janice, Merry Mary, Prompt Paula, Righteous Rhonda, Spiritual Sarah, Timely Tina, Vivacious Vicky, and the game names go on and on.

The game is silently accepted and played without a spoken word. The only rule is to *not* reveal your "true self" in public. Irritability, unhappiness, burn out, fatigue, depression, and the monthly haunting of hormones from month to month must be kept covered with your favorite shades of make up and a smile. Shhhh...it's a secret. No one is allowed to know you are about to reach your breaking point. Just snap in silence.

This is actually a strength women have--to be able to mask our true feelings and go with the flow. In reality, no one really wants to know or needs to know *all* our dirty laundry; however, when the opportunity presents itself to share with another woman, for God's sake, take off your mask!

This is where our power exists--in sharing with each other. However, we forfeit the power with pride and pompous attitudes. Religious women are notorious for this. It is quite comical to watch the saints go marching in for worship with masks on. Don't we attend church seeking hope? Are worshippers not allowed to have a bad day? Isn't this life full of struggles? I thought our struggles are what make us strong and build our character? Well, this is what the preacher said! Some of you may choose to continue snapping in silence, but as for me and my mask, we will unveil and cry out to God for help.

Our most effective encouragement and comfort to others comes from the encouragement and comfort we receive from God in our valley moments.

Not Me!

Okay, I know it's difficult to finally take off the mask and admit you sometimes snap. It is like going on a dinner date without makeup. We all have a breaking point. We all snap. This doesn't mean you are a masked murderer with a dark past. You are simply a loving woman doing the best you can to care for yourself and your family--married or single--with or without children. You may be a perfectionist and keep your house spotless. You may be the owner of a business and respected in your community. You may be a well-loved schoolteacher. You may be active and admired in your church. You may be adjusting to your role as a new mother. You may be a stepmother doing your best to love another woman's children. You may be single and loving it. You do a little today, a little more tomorrow. You give a little today and give a little more tomorrow. You keep going not realizing you have a limit and before you know it, you are exhausted and feeling you can't go on. You push yourself to keep going. You have your game face on and you are playing your part well. This is what we've been taught to do, right? Get up and keep going and going and going. This is what causes us to snap in silence.

Our children have no idea we are so tired that we can hardly walk. Our husbands don't understand *why* we're tired, and we definitely can't share the truth with our co-workers. Nobody knows our fuel tank is low, so what is a woman to do? Play the game! Find the appropriate mask and keep going! You *must* snap in silence because snapping means you are out of control and being out of control is not acceptable--not for you!

Don't you dare admit your plate is full and it's about to crack. Don't you dare share that you are so stressed you can't think straight. You're the glue holding your family together. You are the gas keeping your business running. You are the piece in your church ministry that completes the puzzle. Yes, you appear to have it all together; I commend you for playing the game well.

Let the truth be told; none of us has it all together. We may want to believe we do or want others to believe we do, but we don't. We all have meltdown moments. We occasionally have crying spells not knowing exactly why we cry. We have valley moments and sometimes find it difficult to get back in the game. We all snap in silence. We wait until we're alone and deflate by screaming or crying or just quietly endure.

Some unfortunate family member will be the recipient of unwarranted punishment. An innocent co-worker will accept your irrational behavior. Small incidents may escalate for no reason. Our actions become out of control or we have thoughts of being out of control. Our language may take a turn for the worse. We may even have thoughts of 'touching' our child in a not-so-loving way. Oh, you've never had thoughts like this? May God bless the ground you walk on! Allow me to part the curtains and share a few of my *less than favorable moments.* (That sounds better than the word "snap" doesn't it?)

My thirteen-year-old son is going through puberty and he has a small case of amnesia from time to time. He's almost a different child! His attitude is something I'm not used to and I refuse to tolerate it. The sulking when I tell him to do something does not mix with this mama. One day he made me so angry, I pinned him up against a wall and told him if he didn't straighten up, he would soon be looking at drywall. I snapped.

Now, if my doorbell had rung while I was having this moment with my amnesia-stricken child, I would have answered it with a smile as if nothing was going on. This is what we're supposed to do, right? Always have that mask ready! I should never have gotten to the point of wanting to put my son's head in a wall, but I did. No, he never saw the drywall, but he was afraid!

Allow me to give you another snap scenario through the eyes of a mother. A couple of years ago while running errands with my two sons in the back seat, I lost my temper. The boys were bickering and I was already on edge from being tired and hungry. The bickering was irritating me so much, I couldn't take it anymore--I snapped. While driving, I heatedly reached into the back seat to grab one of them and I pulled my groin muscle. I was in pain, but more angry because they were out of my reach! They weren't acting any differently than any other day in the car, yet this particular day, I couldn't take it. No one knew I lost control except the boys. Good thing there was no hidden camera on the dashboard.

These are the "snap scenario" moments mothers don't share with each other. Why? Shhh... it's a secret. If we told anyone, we might be labeled a "bad mother." Others might even find out we don't have it as together as it appears. Well, it happens to the best of us.

I feel the need to share one more snap scenario because there is a woman reading this who refuses to admit she snaps. Let's visit the area of our life most touchy and secretive--our husbands!

There is nothing I enjoy better than a quiet, relaxing Sunday afternoon. After cooking, eating dinner, and washing the dishes, I gathered books to read and journals to jot notes in while I sat with my husband who was already relaxing and watching a movie. I finally positioned myself on the sofa and exhaled. Out of the blue, my loving husband says to me, "You're a couch potato, you know that?" I couldn't respond because my throat locked up and I felt my brain twisting inside my head thinking about his absurd remark. "Did he just say what I think he said? Does he notice *his* position on the sofa and how long he's been there?" I remembered what time of the month it was, so if I wanted to cut his lips off, I probably could have pled temporary insanity due to a mixture of PMS and peri-menopause. When I didn't respond, he continued to irritate me like a young boy with a crush. He had no idea what he was dealing with as I sat there watching him slowly turn into a green monster that needed to be killed. I thought to myself, "I know he's not crazy, so I must have taken his remark the wrong way." This wasn't my husband after all! Bless his heart; Satan himself was using the father of my children, yet it sure looked like my husband... sounded just like him also!

I could have allowed my home to be disrupted on this beautiful Sunday afternoon, however, I recognized what was going on within me. I checked myself and was able to return to a place of peace in my mind with the help of two of my dearest friends: prayer and meditation. You may not have thoughts so severe, but check your thoughts and actions the next time your husband pushes your buttons or does something he said he'd never do again.

Okay, so you still say your husband or children aren't contributors to meltdown moments? Maybe it's your job or a new business you're trying to get off the ground. Maybe it's your finances or your position in the community sucking the air out of you. You wonder if anyone realizes you're exhausted as they continue to request your time and energy. You wonder if they realize you are only one person. Yet what do you do? Nothing.

Just keep plugging along--doing what you do. It's what everyone expects, so you must deliver. Forget about how you feel. You've performed so well up to this point. It won't look good if you ask for a period of respite. You must maintain your reputation--your performance. You can do it! Just snap in silence.

The Truth Shall Set You Free

Admitting my frustrations and inadequacies as a woman, wife, and mother has truly set me free. What a load to carry, pretending every day is a good day. Once again, I'm not saying we have to open our front door each morning crying for help while others examine our emotions and dirty laundry, but let's be *honest*! Let's be *real*!

As women, we all deal with similar struggles and challenges on different levels, but many times the only things we share with one another are usually the good things. We all at some time feel overwhelmed with the loads we're responsible for. We all deal with laundry, dishes, cooking, careers, ministry, volunteer work, hormones, parents, children, husbands, in-laws, and our own inhibitions, so what's the secret? Keeping up with the mask of the moment is a stressful way to live. Keeping feelings bottled up is enough to cause anyone to snap in silence.

Yes, the truth shall set you free!

I love to have the sweet scent of vanilla and lavender aromatherapy in my home when family and guests enter. Everyone notices the calming, clean smell of my home. Yet if you look under the potpourri pot, a few dust bunnies smile at you!

Parting the Curtains

Why am I parting the curtains and allowing you to look into my life? I have a mentor in San Diego, California, Betty J. Winters, who used the phrase, "*look into my life and learn from it,*" in a six-part series titled, *A Paradigm for Motherhood.* I wondered if another woman could look into my life and learn from it. Can a woman see my life for what it is with my mask on? As a mother of two sons, wife of a loving, high-maintenance husband, and business owner, I'm told quite frequently that I appear to have it all together. Ha! It would be a disservice to God and the planet Earth to accept such a wonderful compliment without sharing the truth, the whole truth, and nothing but the truth. I am far from having it all together, yet I've learned to play the game well--quite well.

Nevertheless, I'm sick and tired of playing. I'm tired of having to look the part of the professional Momsweb founder and chipper home-schooling mom. I don't even know what that woman is supposed to look like; I can only be myself, and not what society says I'm supposed to be. I'm a jean and t-shirt, occasional skirt-wearing mama with an attitude. I love my Jesus, love my time alone, and I'm tired of playing the game. My secret is out, and to the many wives and mothers still playing the game, your secret should become unveiled also. Part those curtains! Knowing someone may be helped makes it easier to part *my* curtains.

Exposing my life is my way of letting women know we may not speak a universal language in regards to our roles as wives and mothers and we may not have the same values and ideas, yet we share common groundwork: a home to keep, children to raise, some type of hormonal issue (whether we flow each month or not). We definitely all get tired, and for those who are married, we have matrimony music to dance to.

The goal of this book is for women to collectively come to the realization that it is okay to have a bad day every now and then; we all have a breaking point. It's okay to admit our inadequacies as a wife and mother--no one is perfect. It's okay to feel tired and say it--we all need a break. It's okay to voice not always feeling loved by your husband--they can't give us the love we want. It's okay to get sick of your children every now and then--it's their job to make you sick. Really, it's okay!

Voicing these thoughts only shows we have the wisdom to share, be honest, and are open to receive help, if we desire help. Sometimes women just need an outlet. In a weird way, venting releases energy to go on. It's like a cleansing process. We're clearing out unwanted cobwebs from our mind. How are we supposed to find the support we need if we never share our true emotions? I think it is great to *appear* to have it all together as long as we are honest with ourselves and with others--when necessary. How can we encourage one another if we aren't truthful about the joys *and* struggles we experience? I'm sharing the reality of womanhood, of motherhood: the pleasures and pains, the struggles and liberations, the tears and the fulfillments, and the ingredients to living in perfect peace--everyday.

Having a transparent life is definitely not my choice, yet it is my calling. It's amazing how God has used my dirt to heal another heart--he wants to use yours also. The first time I heard the phrase, "look into my life and learn from it," I knew this would be my avenue to share peace with women. I definitely couldn't write about something I know nothing about. I *KNOW* peace! How do I know peace? I know peace by knowing what isn't peace: by going through some storms, by feeling like I was losing my mind, by snapping again and again in silence. I've had some dark moments in my life as a woman, some hopeless nights as a wife, and some disturbing moments as a mother, but I'm still here. Peace is my promise of hope. Knowing peace has changed me and is still changing me.

I refer to peace as my best friend. Peace is what keeps me from day to day. Peace is my sanity. Peace is my fortress. Peace is my fresh air. Peace is my personal space hidden in the corner of my mind. Peace is private. Peace is my free, never-ending retreat. Peace is perfect.

Woman/Wife/Mother

Woman, wife, *then* mother: this sequence must never change and if it does, a woman becomes out of sync--out of balance. If you ever feel like something just isn't right with you, begin by checking your order. Is the woman in you first in your life? Before the wife or mother is reached, the woman must be accessed. It is the woman who defines the wife and mother. It is the woman who sets the tone for the character of the wife and mother. It is the woman who decides if the wife will be satisfied and if the mother will be content. It is the woman who gives permission to live a life of peace.

If you haven't acknowledged the woman in you, stop for a minute and look in the mirror. You were a woman before you became a wife. You were a woman before you became a mother. Many of us have lost *ourselves,* so first we must find that woman and learn to love her. You have wants, needs, and desires as a woman. You have purpose. You have value.

If the first thing you do when you open your eyes in the morning is change a diaper, you're out of sync. Yes, those cuddly, helpless bundles of joy somehow find themselves at the top of the chain, yet they too have their place. With the numerous responsibilities calling for a woman's attention every day, rising early and pouring into ourselves on a daily basis is a necessity; it is a prerequisite to being whole and feeling complete.

To the new moms who don't have the pleasure of rising early because you are never getting to sleep, get it whenever you can until you learn to juggle those two free minutes. Our sequence of woman/wife/mother is often kept out of order. Many women have become comfortable with a backward sequence. This is partly why our lives are without peace. Balance allows peace to surface.

My second-born often asks why I awake so early in the mornings. My reply is always, "I need to take care of mama, so that mama can take care of you."

My Baby Doll

Most of us were given at least one doll as a little girl. We loved our doll and cared for her with pride. We clothed her, fed her, bathed her, and put her to sleep. In our very early years, this doll helped sharpen our already natural nurturing ability. We were taught to care for others and we loved doing it. Many of us had an Easy Bake oven and toy dishes that we were excited about washing. Playing "house" was fun. Where was the programming to care for and love ourselves? There wasn't any. When were we taught to make ourselves happy and to focus on our wellbeing? We weren't.

Is it wrong to teach a young girl to nurture herself and make herself number one? I know this is blasphemy to many women (to put yourself before your family), yet as you continue reading, you'll find it's selfish to *not* put yourself before your family. It's time for a little de-programming.

Most of us can't see or realize our own needs because we're suffocated with everyone else's needs. We have subtle feelings of guilt when we do something for ourselves. Sometimes our family will thicken the guilt layer by acting completely incapable of surviving without us. It is a great feeling to be needed, but this warm, fuzzy feeling can be crippling to the family and damaging to us.

Woman/wife/mother: let's briefly survey these three heavy loads of life. These aren't our only loads, yet they are by far the heaviest and most demanding. We also carry the loads of being a daughter, sister, friend, and many more!

Load I--A Woman

A woman is an extra-special being. I don't think I could handle knowing the magnitude of my value and need on Earth. I believe the world would crumble without women. I'm blessed to have a father who not only told me, but showed me my value as a woman. He always says to give little girls all the love and cuddling they can get while they're young because when they get older and marry, it's all over--women become the cuddle-givers! It's important that women and men show little girls their value and importance at a young age because the day will come when they wonder if they are appreciated, valued, or even wanted.

It can be quite painful when those you love (husband and children) take you for granted; however, remembering those early words of encouragement and validity as a young girl will surface and a woman will be capable of encouraging herself.

If you did not receive this love and cuddling as a child, here is your dose. Can you imagine the world without women? The world would not be replenished without women. The world needs women to create balance and stability in the home. The world needs women to maintain peace and harmony. The world needs women to stand by, encourage, and hold up the men in our country wanting and needing our help. The world needs feminine comfort and woman's natural nurturing abilities.

You play a part in making an impact on the nation-- beginning in your home. You are an important being on the planet Earth. No pressure, but there is no time for pity parties! Yes, we all experience pain; yet there is power in our pain and pain produces character and strength. I am WOMAN! You are WOMAN! We are WOMEN! Yes, we have much to bear--this is our calling. We are expected to be everything to everybody, and we hold within us the power and resources to do what needs to be done. Not using our natural resources is a sure ticket to failure.

God has an exceptionally funny sense of humor. Who in their right mind would ask one woman to wear several different hats at the same time, multi task, and wish there were more hours in the day? A manager, cook, coach, nurturer, cheerleader, taxi-driver, accountant, project organizer, nurse, caretaker, teacher, housekeeper, mediator, advisor, counselor and if you're really lucky, you get to meet the physical needs of a loving husband and don the hat of sex goddess! Only a supernatural God would put this on anyone--man is not capable of thinking of or creating such an intricate being. I choose to believe God doesn't make mistakes, so since He has placed these multiple roles on women, He has also given us every tool, resource, and quality we need to fulfill our role and fill it to the optimum level--with peace of mind.

Women truly are extraordinary beings. There is a power in us we haven't realized yet - a power we haven't discovered. My husband constantly says, "Women have the power." It's funny how men *know* we hold the power, yet we still haven't learned *how* to exercise it. Once we realize our power lies between our lips and not in our hips, we'll really have it going on! We have the power to control and influence. We have the ability to mold minds!

If we have all this power, why do we struggle at something as simple as keeping our peace of mind? Why does it seem like we have the weight of the world on our shoulders? Why do we endure constant inner turmoil? Why do we have these unwelcome melting moments which cause us to snap? The world was not complete until God created woman. So, if we are so vital and valued, why do we often feel incomplete?

What a Man Thinks

Wouldn't it be nice to get inside a man's mind and find out what he really thinks of a woman? Well, my dear father has shared quite a few secrets with me. His candid sharing about men has helped me to understand and appreciate my husband more. I'll never forget the story he told me about the woman and the apple tree. Maybe this is where the superwoman mentality comes from?

It goes like this. A man desires an apple pie. He expects his woman to climb the apple tree fully dressed, with nails impeccably manicured and hair neatly combed. She is expected to climb the apple tree like a lady, pick the best apples, and climb back down the tree looking as good as she did when she climbed up. Her hair should still be in place with no nails chipped. Full of energy and bubbly as ever, she is expected to willingly bake the apple pie from scratch and serve it to her man with a smile. If this isn't an example of superwoman, I don't know what is! Some of us are crazy enough to try to uphold this image and appear to always have it together.

Now, I try to look decent for my husband when he comes home from work. After being at home with the children all day, I can get pretty raggedy, so some effort goes into looking good for my husband--thanks to my father. When I had my first child over twelve years ago, Daddy told me not to wear t-shirts with the baby's spit up on my shoulders when I greet my husband. (Back then, I didn't care if I had boo-boo on my lap, but now I understand the importance of this small act of kindness for my man.)

A man once told me that if he came back into the world, he'd come back as a woman. Not only do I wish I could grant his wish, yet I hope the day he comes back, he's on his period and cramping, a baby on his hip, dishes to be washed, loads of laundry to fold and put away, and a husband barely making minimum wage coming home and asking, "What's for dinner?" Ha! Please come back as a woman!

Load II--A Wife

If I knew saying, "I do" meant agreeing to painful life lessons to prune, change, and rearrange my character and strengthen my ability to love, I would have never walked down the aisle. Well, if I didn't walk down the aisle, I would not be who I am today. If I had not walked down the aisle, I would not have married my Sugar Bear: my husband. Yes, love is blind and thank God it is. I love my Sugar Bear, yet the bear is not always full of sugar - neither am I. Nobody warned me of the truths of marriage, and I am almost positive I told someone to step on my wedding dress train if they saw me making my way down the aisle. Whomever I asked to save me, didn't. They probably would not have succeeded anyway because I was in love and I still am.

The love is now stronger and unlike our early years, I no longer wonder if I married the right man. The love has strengthened to allow us to stand the tests of marriage. The love is deeper to help me accept Sugar Bear just as he is. My marriage trials and triumphs have truly helped mold me into a more loving, supportive, helpmate.

This doesn't mean my marriage is perfect. We are far from perfect and still have trying times, but I'm wiser, stronger, and understand love and humility more. I also understand the importance of being a forgiving wife. Women are called to be the man's helpmate, yet we can hardly help ourselves. I remember being so exhausted one night and falling asleep on the sofa, as I often do. It took my last ounce of energy to peel myself off the sofa to get in the shower and go to bed. While standing under the warm water, I realized only a supernatural power could have helped me off the sofa and into the shower. Not my husband, not my children, not my mother or my father, not even my own "can do" attitude--nothing but the supernatural power of God. Once wives realize husbands are incapable of fulfilling and meeting all our needs, we will be more content in our marriages.

Helpmate? I take this literally. Our men need our help, yet we came into the marriage hoping they could help us a little also. We expected them to make us happy and keep us occupied. My Mother gave me a piece of advice when I married that has been worth more than gold. I pass this gold on to every new bride when the opportunity arises. Her advise was, "Don't depend on your husband to make you happy." During the first few years of my marriage, I didn't think mama's advice applied to me. After all, my groom was different, which was why I married him! Sugar Bear was everything I wanted in a man. I was happy and in love. After a few years of marriage, something changed. My *man* was still everything I wanted, yet he became my *husband*. He was doing his best, yet I expected and demanded more. As far as I was concerned--he changed.

Ditch the Dream

My unrealistic expectations of my husband took me to a pool of dissatisfaction and I began to ask the question, "What happened?" Not only were these expectations unfair to him, they were damaging our marriage. I began planning my dream wedding when I was in high school by purchasing brides books and imagining exactly what my wedding would be like. Little emphasis was put on my marriage because all my attention was on the wedding ceremony. I had a dream and expected my husband to *help* make my dream come true. He didn't have a chance! I set him up for failure from the very beginning. When I shared my feelings of discontent with him, he was confused.

Most husbands don't understand a wife's feelings of disappointment in a marriage. They don't understand what the problem is and as far as they are concerned, everything is just fine! Why wouldn't they think everything is fine? They have someone always available to help them with whatever they need. I too, would think everything was all right if someone was cooking my meals, washing my clothes, encouraging me, and answering when I called! Everything would be GREAT!

Because of our dissatisfaction and our husband's inability to comprehend our feelings, we snap in silence. We begin to have private arguments with our spouse in our minds, our actions reveal our disgust, and before we know it, our marriage has gone beyond sour, yet no one will ever know. This is when the mask is most important. A marriage gone bad is not acceptable; therefore, we look for quick getaways to heal our broken hearts. Malls, retreats, friends, food, or whatever will help mask the emotion. Shhh…it's a secret.

Meanwhile, our husbands appear to still enjoy the matrimony bliss, while we wonder if they are in the same marriage with us. We wonder why we are married, but feeling lonely. Because we have depended on our groom to make us happy, we throw out statements such as:

- "You don't take me out anymore."
- "You never compliment me."
- "You don't love me anymore."
- "You don't help out around the house."
- "You don't spend enough time with the children."
- "You spend too much time with your friends."
- "You need to check your priorities."
- "You need to be a man."
- "I feel like a single parent."

I'm sure you can come up with a few of your own, yet doesn't it sound like we're pointing the finger at the husband? Even if the statements *are* true, why is our husband our focus? Have you ever noticed your husband's reaction to various situations are completely different from yours? Yes, men are a little different and that's the way they are wired, so we have to stop trying to change him! It's the nature of the beast--no pun intended.

Don't forget, the same man sleeping on the sofa in front of the television or working late hours is the same handsome, fun-loving man you were proud to marry. He's still your man, yet he became your husband and you became his wife. He's not giving you the attention you think you deserve? Is he responsible for making you happy? No, you can't depend on another person to make you happy. *You are responsible for your own happiness.* Is he responsible for keeping you occupied? No, but it sure would be nice to be courted again, right? Yet remember, he became a husband and now he needs *your* help--in every aspect.

I began to have peace in my marriage when I divorced the unfair, destructive thoughts in my mind about my husband and focused on what made me fall in love with him. Yes, sometimes you have to go back that far--the beginning.

Men marry for many reasons, as do women. One of their reasons is to have someone help them. Whether they need help emotionally, physically, spiritually, or mentally...they need help, so your husband married you. If you aren't sure how to help him, ask him! Wife is my name, customer service is my game.

Just as a Mother is protective of her child, God is protective of these men. Our husband--His son. To treat him any way other than loving is quite hurtful. No, I'm not taking his side; I have a husband also. The day I realized Sugar Bear was someone's son I had been judging, unforgiving, and unloving towards, I changed. I had to release the negative thoughts in my head and look in the mirror--ouch!

As Mama frequently says to me, "Girl, you better pop your skirt and keep walking!" Mama's statement means I must go on with my life regardless of another person's actions or words. I have to shake some stuff off and keep moving. Waddling in the mud over another person's wrongs only keeps me from moving forward. Thank you, Mama! In the end, husbands and wives will be held accountable. As a wife, I can only do my part and I will do my part. Sugar Bear has to answer for himself.

I remember calling my mother one day to ask her how to bake an apple pie. When Daddy answered the phone, I knew Mama wasn't at home. I remember Daddy cooking as a little girl and he made a mean omelet, so I was sure he could help me; so I asked him. I'll never forget Daddy's reply. "Why do I need to know how to make an apple pie? That's why I got married!" Although we both laughed, there was much truth in his statement.

What About Me?

I hear you. What about us? Women seem to be the primary givers in relationships. Well, we are taken care of as we do our part in helping those placed in our lives. Peace and contentment surfaced in my marriage when I cancelled the "what about me" parties. No one ever accepted my invitations anyway!

The phrase, 'behind every man is a good woman', has truth. For the single women wondering if Mr. Right is out there, yes he is. He may not appear like Mr. Right, but he is out there. You may be the kiss of life a confused frog is waiting for.

We are helpmates; help him! Don't nag him; help him! Don't criticize him; help him! No man is without an issue-- alcohol, drugs, pornography, wondering eyes, rubber necks, sloppiness, lack of table manners, foul language, couch potato, bed potato, egotistical attitude, workaholic, controlling or just plain lazy--pick one, or two, or more. A perfect man does not exist.

Once I set Sugar Bear free to live in his own world and not mine, my job as his wife became easier. I was no longer the self-appointed judge assigned to point out his faults. Oftentimes, a woman is needed to help these hidden diamonds through their rough stages. We are the buffer to help them shine--to help them become the man they want to be. Yes, it takes much compassion, patience, understanding, and humility, yet I'm a witness: your diamond is worth it.

The more I humble myself and put Sugar Bear's needs first without having a "what about me" attitude, the more considerate Sugar Bear is of my needs. If I slack up, he slacks up. If I stop, he stops. I'm a witness; endurance pays off. I once heard a minister say at a wedding, "out-serve your spouse." Someone has got to initiate small acts of kindness. Someone has got to show love when the other is acting unlovable. Someone has got to show humility. Okay, let's put it plainly. Someone has got to be the one to temporarily sacrifice their needs and be willing to be used by God. Will it be you or will you ask, "What about me?"

I contemplated leaving my marriage a few times...thank God I didn't because I would have missed seeing my diamond shine. Watching the process can seem never ending and can be painful, yet it is worth the wait. When we learn not to focus on our husband's faults and shortcomings, peace will surface. It may sound backward, but it works. I chose my words carefully regarding the matter of marriage; nevertheless, I want to share the reality. Marriage is not a fairy tale. It's not all about the ceremony. It's about the long walk down the aisle to say, "I do." "I do" to a life lesson on love, humility, sacrifice, and patience. Don't forget, sharing your story may strengthen another woman.

For those women in abusive relationships, as I was before I met Sugar Bear, I'll share with you what my father says, "Leave or learn to die well." Whether you are succumbed to physical, verbal, or mental abuse, I pray you will love yourself enough to know you deserve to be treated no less than royalty--you too, are God's child. If you don't love yourself, no one else will.

Load III--A Mother

Don't stop reading because you haven't given birth. If you have ever poured any part of yourself into a child's life you have mothered. If you desire to be a mother, know a mother, or if you have a mother, this load is for you also. What will it take to understand the true value of a mother? What will it take before mothers are appreciated for their true worth? Until a mother learns to appreciate herself, understand her value in the home, and learns that taking care of herself *first* makes her a better person, no one else can be expected to understand or appreciate our God-given value. It takes a mother to understand a mother. We will soon learn to stop seeking appreciation, affirmation, and kudos from those who don't understand what we go through.

Our family sees what we do, yet at the same time and through those same eyes, they *don't* see what we do. They just don't get it! They don't think we get sick, tired, or sick and tired! Do you think they keep expecting us to give if they really understood how we felt? I choose to believe my family is not that insensitive. I have accepted the fact they aren't able to fully comprehend my role and responsibilities. My goodness! I'm just beginning to understand my role and responsibilities, and I've been a mother for twelve-plus years.

I didn't capture the true essence of motherhood until I found out I had a bone tumor in my femur. The tumor was benign, yet potent enough to change my life - completely. My defining moment of motherhood birthed my website Momsweb. I realized the need for this book through Momsweb. While sharing the reality of my life as a wife and mother, other women began to privately share their stories. They too, admitted the secret and felt alone with their mixed emotions concerning the heavy loads we bear. No more secrets.

I wished someone had shared more with me before I was married with children. A mother holds the most valuable, influential position in the world. A mother's job requires top multi tasking expertise, yet no training is available--only on the job training.

May God bless the young girls with older women in their life that will *be there* when needed. Women are charged with raising future generations with morals and values. We are responsible for teaching solid character qualities, while at the same time, our character is being formed. We are strategically chosen to raise the children in our care. What an awesome, yet demanding position to be placed in! Mothers have dominion over the children of the world. We are pulled in every direction and exhausted of all energy. Being a mother is the highest calling and we are exceptionally rewarded when we properly fill the position.

A breaking point accompanies this high calling that *must* be acknowledged. Every mother experiences bad days including the woman who encourages and inspires you the most. She is full of encouraging words and inner strength because she has experienced her share of unpleasant days and has begun the path to experiencing perfect peace in the midst of her chaotic days. No mother is excluded. The mother at the park, the soccer mom, the home schooling mother, the PTA mom, the wealthy mom, the working mom, the entrepreneur mom, the single mom, the step mom, the pretty mom, the aerobics mom, the eccentric mom, and even the mom who leads her family to church each time the church doors are open--we all have a breaking point. News flash: being a mother is not an easy job!

Now that our secret has been exposed and we know we have a breaking point, why is there a need to mask our frustrations? What exactly is the secret? What is the fear in picking up the phone to call another woman to say, "I feel like I'm about to snap!" Fear of rejection? Fear of being criticized, judged, or maybe even talked about? Maybe we feel it is okay to snap in silence since everyone else does from time to time. Why talk about it? Allow me to part the curtains and reveal a few of my own inadequacies and frustrations as a mother.

My New Assignment

After retiring from the military, I was extremely excited about retiring to be home with my two sons. Unbeknownst to me, there were more than a few things in store for me I was not prepared for. I was hesitant about sharing my motherhood troubles, so I kept them to myself. After all, I was a military woman trained to adapt and adjust, surely I can handle this. After twenty years of structure and discipline in the Navy, I struggled with my daily motherly role--I questioned my natural ability. Two years into my retirement, I thought I was losing my mind. My *plan of the day* wasn't working the way it did in the Navy. I started to understand why some women preferred to work outside the home. I found myself weighing the pros and cons of being at home and wondered if I made the right decision.

While in the Navy, regardless of how hectic my workday was; my job was my time away from the homefront.

Although my real job (my family) didn't begin until after an exhausting day outside the home, I still had time away. I wondered if I was the only mother loaded down by laundry, victimized by the vacuum, and distracted by dirty dishes; I was held hostage by housework! I joined a mothers group online to get to know some other women and from the sound of the emails, they were living a life of relaxation and planning play days! Forget the play days; I wanted a support group! Was I the only one looking for support? Did I have a problem? Was I the only one feeling this way? Help! I don't feel like cooking everyday- as a matter of fact, I don't like to cook at all! Where is all this laundry coming from? Are my children placing clean clothes in the dirty clothes hamper to avoid hanging them up? Am I the official dish-washer? What's up with these toilets? I cleaned toilets in the Navy; I'm retired now, why am I still doing it? Where do these stories come from my children are telling me? I had no idea they had such an imagination! Is there a limit to how many I have to listen to on a daily basis? Give me a break! Where is the relief?

Besides being a mother, can we talk about being a wife?

Does my husband realize I'm his help*mate* and not his help*maid*? I felt stretched in all directions and felt alone until one day I got brave enough to express my feelings. I boldly shared myself with a few mothers and BEHOLD, most were experiencing the same inadequate feelings! What was the big secret? Why haven't I ever heard about this side of motherhood?

I was around many stay-at-home mothers before I retired, and all I remember hearing was, "You'll see!" See what? Was this a part of some initiation process for being a mother? Why isn't this discussed as a natural part of motherhood?

Who are we keeping the secrets from? One mother asked me why it was necessary to reveal and discuss our bad days. Just think, if I had never opened my mouth to share, others would not have opened up. I would have continued thinking I was alone in my feelings of failure. I am hardly alone. Sharing the experience of a bad day may help another have a good day. Sharing offers hope. Sharing offers comfort as a listening mother realizes she is not alone.

My days are coated with prayer. I prepare myself for unexpected bumpy moments that creep up throughout the day, but I still fall short--really short. Yes, I bounce back. I *must* bounce back. When I feel a pity party coming on because I feel used and abused by my family, I immediately turn my focus off of them and onto me. We naturally go after those closest to us when we want some extra love and attention. Trust me--unless you tell them exactly what to do and when, you'll grow frustrated and angry because they aren't giving you what you need. As I mentioned before, they don't know what we need. They don't understand our role, so what are we waiting for? Do something for yourself! I like waiting for everyone to go to bed to enjoy my favorite dessert--alone. I may take a long, hot shower or exercise while nobody is watching. If I so desire, I may just sit and look at the walls. Whatever I want to do for myself, I do it. Tears heal and strengthen, yet we have to find other ways to fulfill and encourage ourselves. If we don't, the day will come when you snap in silence.

Allow me to part the curtains again and share a frightening experience I had with my first-born. My husband and I were completing some last-minute packing to prepare for a drive across-country. He always manages to finish packing first and being the mighty man he is, he was ready to load the car! "Time to go! Are you ready?" Am I ready? I wasn't close to being finished packing for me and first-born, who was about six months old or younger. He was lying on the bed crying, probably hungry, and surrounded by mounds of clothes waiting to be packed. What will I need to drive across country with a baby? Will the weather change? Do I take bottles already prepared or make them on the road? How many clothes? What about me? Where are my clothes? I couldn't think straight.

The baby was crying and my husband was ready to go. Sugar Bear came into the room to get my bags and I remember saying to him, "I don't have it all together right now. I may have a chemical imbalance, so if you want your baby, get him or he'll be smothered in all these clothes and NO I'm not ready!" I said it very calmly and now that I think back, I should have screamed and acted like the crazy woman I felt like. I probably would have received more of a reaction from Sugar Bear. He did what he knew to do. He picked up our baby and saved him from his crazy mama.

Oh, how I wished he had picked me up and comforted me instead of first-born. Instead, I was left alone to deal with my emotions. Sugar Bear didn't know how to relate to me. I probably scared him because I was supposed to be his strong "helper." As a new mother, I didn't feel allowed to have weak moments and I didn't know how to ask for help, so I snapped. The sad part of this story is my husband doesn't remember this very dark moment in my life.

I wonder how many new mothers experience these melting moments and have no one to share with. It's sad to me how we host baby showers and overwhelm mothers-to-be with gifts, yet we don't share the ultimate gift--the truth--the reality of motherhood. Why don't we talk about post-partum depression and sleep deprivation? What kind of women are we to *not* share these things with each other? Oh yeah, I forgot... we're playing the game of charades. Shhh! We'll just let these new mothers snap in silence.

Once we realize we are all susceptible to having bad days, we might not be so hard on ourselves. A perfect mother does not exist. It's good to assess our role every now and then as long as we don't try to measure and compare to another mother... remember, meet yourself where *you* are and make changes according to what works for *your* family--*your* life--*your* household. Mothers are good for sizing each other up. We judge each other on our decisions, how we dress, coping skills, career choices, transportation, financial status, education and any other life choice we can find. What matters most is our responsibility to raise and nurture the children entrusted in our care: whether they are in our home, or whether they are those with whom we are fortunate to cross paths.

We are so self-absorbed. We tend to think everything we go through is about us. Remember, our pain is power--when shared. Our pain is another woman's gain.

My Pathway to Peace

Now that we have examined the three heavy loads of our life, what is the recipe to experiencing peace within each role? It isn't a secret. It's something we've heard most of our adult life, yet we struggle with it daily.

One Mother's Day with my mother and younger sister, I asked my mother what piece of advice she would give to mothers. She said "Peace. Don't let anyone or anything steal your peace of mind. Not *perfect* peace, just have some peace!" My Mother is an icon of peace. Growing up, I remember friends and family coming by saying how peaceful the house was--not quiet, yet peaceful.

Her environment is always peaceful; it isn't the house, it is her being. Peace oozes from my mother's pores. Her peace is transferred throughout her home. She mastered the ability to be at peace in any circumstance. My father was in the Navy, so he was away from home a lot. Mama was left to keep three girls plus her youngest sister she was raising. Mama was a true home-keeper awaiting Daddy's homecomings. She somehow did it without allowing her feathers to be publicly fluttered.

Hmmm... was mama playing the game of charades or did she sincerely have peace? There *is* a difference, you know. Now that I'm a grown woman, wife, and mother, I can definitely say my mother was showing peace.

I invite you into my meeting room, the kitchen, which is where I first found peace. The kitchen is my least favorite aspect of domestic work, yet I find the kitchen to be a quiet place, a retreat, because no one wants to clean it up--this means I can be alone. Washing dishes has been one of my ways to have time alone and I've done this long before I was married. Now that I'm married with children, the kitchen is my family's designated meeting place. I seem to spend most of my time in the kitchen, so I still use it as my place of peace. If I need my sons or husband to disappear, I simply ask for help cleaning!

One frustrating day while in the kitchen washing dishes, it occurred to me that I don't have the luxury to purchase a one-way ticket out of the city when life isn't going my way. I had to find peace in the midst of my chaos and I did. I also wanted to find peace for the many mothers not able to pack up and attend a weekend retreat due to finances, children, or other reasons. My God *promised* me perfect peace, so I tested it.

Over the course of two years, several changes were made in my life that not only gave me peace, yet more joy, harmony in my home, and acceptance of myself. I had more patience with my children, love for my husband, and a higher appreciation for myself. Nothing changed except me: my attitude, my disposition, and my thoughts. I came up with a daily maintenance checklist of items I needed to maintain my peace of mind.

Because the kitchen was where I found peace, I refer to this checklist as my recipe. These ingredients in the recipe will not stand alone. They must be mixed properly to withstand the daily battles of life. The checklist is titled **PMS: Preventive Maintenance of Self.**

PMS

I've dealt with PMS most of my life and it's not a fun experience, especially when everyone around you thinks it is all in your head. Well, this is a new form of PMS and it's completely opposite to the one we're so familiar with. I'm proud to have it and so will every other woman. Our new and improved PMS is titled Preventive Maintenance of Self.

Most of us know our true selves and really aren't proud of who we are when we unmask, thus, another reason for the charades game. I can be an ugly, selfish, and mean woman, and one of my daily prayers is for God to hide me from myself. I was tired of my moody days and lack of control with the everyday matters of life. I needed to find a way to prevent getting to the snapping point. My answer to my prayer was PMS--Preventive Maintenance from Self. PMS helped find a balance for my temperament.

As I began to incorporate PMS into my daily life, I realized my ugliness is only revealed when my maintenance checklist is neglected. My feathers are easily ruffled when my checklist is not adhered to.

PMS is a list of ingredients that must be poured into the mix of my life - daily. Not one ingredient may be omitted from the mix. There is no peace package to purchase, no membership fees, or equipment costs. All you need is yourself and a desire to experience fulfillment as a woman, wife, and mother. I challenge you to join me on a proven pathway to perfect peace.

Life is like a cake. The ingredients alone have little appreciation, yet when mixed together, the finished product is gratifying and the flavor is hard to resist.

Encourage Yourself!

The first ingredient in our recipe is encouragement. Everyone needs encouragement and a woman is definitely no exception. Being a wife and mother takes a toll on a woman, and even minimal recognition has the capability of giving us the strength to go on. Employees are encouraged for their jobs done well, students get recognized for accomplishments, sports teams are definitely encouraged to continue performance, and even babies are encouraged as they make milestones in their developmental stages. Unfortunately, women feel invisible in the home and crave for an occasional thank you, a bouquet of flowers, a chance to be served dinner, or just a few minutes of peace and quiet-- ALONE.

We don't always receive these small treasures, therefore, we must learn to love, recognize, and encourage ourselves. Not feeling appreciated by our family can draw us into a web of sorrows and it's impossible to see good in anything and anybody. Fatigue, hormones, hunger, chemical imbalances, and mood swings are just a few things that exasperate our emotions. Feeling unloved and unappreciated can make us want to paint the walls in our home black; we have the power to do this without opening one can of paint.

Women experience days where happiness can not be found. Becoming easily frustrated and fed up with life is common and these feelings overtake our minds quickly. Before you know it, we've said or done something we wish we could take back. Some women wish they could go back in time and never have married or had children at all. You may not have experienced these extreme feelings, but we have all experienced valley moments and wondered if anyone cared.

It is essential to our well-being that we learn to encourage ourselves. We must pour into ourselves as we so willingly pour into others. Our telephone can ring with a problem on the other end, and we'll have the perfect words to uplift and encourage, yet as soon as we fall into our own pit of sorrow, we beat ourselves up. We should love ourselves better.

How do you encourage yourself? This answer may be different for every woman, so we must first recognize the value in who we are as women. Forget the wife and mother role for a minute and concentrate on you.

God created you with no mistakes. You were perfectly created with purpose. There is no one else like you and no one can do what you were created to do. No one can touch the lives you will touch. No one thinks like you or has the ideas and creativity you do. You are extraordinary just by being you. Recognize your value in the home. Recognize how much you're needed. How can we expect others to appreciate and recognize us when we don't appreciate and recognize ourselves? We expect our husband to do things for us we won't do for ourselves. We seek the approval from our family when they can't begin to understand what we do and who we are. We set ourselves up for disappointment.

Start speaking encouraging words to yourself right now!

At the end of each day as I lay my head on my pillow, I consider the day's events. While listening to the quietness of the house, I assure myself I've done only what I could and I did my best--regardless if anyone else noticed. I'm in a unique position to encourage other women, which makes me require frequent encouragement refills. When I feel myself needing to be encouraged, I focus on that need. Allowing my mind to visit areas of my life with which I'm not satisfied only worsens my attitude. Ladies, do what you have to do--do whatever it takes! Meditate, pray, sing, dance, or buy yourself a gift.

Before I married, I allowed negative words to control me. Controlling boyfriends tried and almost succeeded in stripping me of my confidence and self-esteem. They obviously saw my hidden power, yet I did not.

We can also verbally abuse ourselves by not speaking words of affirmation to ourselves. Love yourself!

Accept yourself! Encourage yourself! If you have to--talk to yourself!

If we didn't have the ability to compare, we'd be satisfied with who we are--let's stop looking at others and look in the mirror with acceptance. If you don't like what you see, only *you* can do something about it. You can't blame anyone except yourself.

Mother's Day and birthdays wouldn't be so disappointing if we loved ourselves and encouraged ourselves on a daily basis. As I grow older and comprehend the power in speaking wholesome words to myself, I have more peace. Words of comfort allow peace of mind to surface. If talking to yourself doesn't work for you, try remembering there is always someone worse off than you. Whether you believe it or not, there is someone who would love to be in your shoes right now. Someone would appreciate your situation more than you do! Whenever you feel the need to send invitations to your next pity party; think of someone you know having a troublesome time in their life. You may not be all you want to be in your life, your husband's priorities may be completely different from yours, and your children may be taking a path different from the five-year plan you had set for them, but you can experience peace right where you are.

There have been instances in my life where God was either going to show me the reality of peace or I was going to lose my mind--literally. Before I found peace, I didn't feel loved by my husband or children. I felt used, abused, and unappreciated. I knew this wasn't how I was supposed to go through life, so I began my path to find perfect peace--I wasn't going to be satisfied with just peace. I wanted perfect peace as promised to me by God.

Each morning during my meditation, I thank God for the simple ability to be. Not what I am or what I do, just the ability to be. Allowing my God to fill this vessel with the ability to be gives me other abilities--the ability to teach, mold, train, encourage, and so much more. I encourage you to begin your own self-encouraging ritual.

Pray or Meditate!

Women will hit the floor running in the morning and not stop until they return to their bed at night. Having a busy day is enough reason to spend quality time in prayer and/or meditation. Although women from various spiritual beliefs are reading, prayer and meditation are closely related. I hope we can agree we all need some type of prayer/meditation in our life to have peace. When a busy day is ahead of us, we truly can't afford not to coat it in prayer and meditation. Even *with* prayer, our days can become hectic, so beginning the day without it only invites unwanted stress and struggles which begin as soon as we open our eyes. I find myself able to deal with the day's mishaps a lot better when I'm covered in prayer.

Meditating takes me to another place--the place of perfect peace. Meditating reminds me I am powerless without God. I need His strength and power poured into me to get through the day. The key is to stay connected to our source of power and strength. Trying to survive on our own energy is a ticket to burnout.

Immediately after my prayer/meditation time, I feel empowered. I feel I can conquer the world. Having a praying/meditating spirit throughout the day is a secret weapon. It doesn't matter if you work outside the home or in the home, staying connected will prevent short fuses. Staying connected will help deal with spilled milk. Staying connected will help you recognize that sweating the small stuff is a waste of energy, and energy is something we can't afford to waste! Life's situations can easily block our connection--that's life.

Before you know it, our mind is completely consumed with the one situation we're dealing with. We've turned a single matter into a major thought process and that's all we think about. We continually revisit situations that bothered us or play back hurting words in our mind from a loved one. We call friends about it, cry about it, complain and grumble about it and guess what? You are the only one who really cares about it.

We've allowed ourselves to unplug from our power source. Think for a minute how much time is spent on things we can't change. We spend a lot of time trying to figure out or correct the past-- impossible. "Why did he do this?" "Why didn't they do that?" "What is wrong with them?" Developing a praying spirit prevents our mind from becoming a dump.

RIP--React In Peace!

One of the greatest benefits of prayer/meditation is being able to maintain a constant peace of mind - no matter what happens, what circumstances occur, and what is going on around us. Mama always told me not to let what people do surprise me. This is better said than done, yet as I get older I realize how beneficial her statement is to my peace of mind. Having the ability to RIP--React in Peace--to the comments and actions of others is a treasure. Our treasure is our peace.

Women have different degrees of coping skills and we react to life circumstances in various ways. Comparing yourself or judging another woman's reaction to a situation is dangerous. Not only do we set ourselves up for feelings of inadequacy, it's completely unfair. You haven't walked in her shoes or lived in her home. What constitutes an emergency to her may be *just* a part of everyday life to you. Do you fall to pieces when you receive news of a family illness or death? Do you fly off the handle when you walk into your child's room and it looks like a trash dump? Do you run around aimlessly with no direction when you're running late for an appointment? How do you respond when your husband isn't accountable?

Our stressful moments are defining moments of our character. Every woman has a button to be pushed which causes her to lose her temper, have a bad day, or become frustrated. Yes, even the woman you call on for an encouraging word. As previously mentioned, she has had a few melting moments and has learned how to handle unexpected events and emergencies in her life.

I'm often told of how calm I react to particular situations. After feeling ridiculous for reacting to trifling matters and people, I've learned to just go with the flow. I've circled so many drains over *light afflictions* only to find out they work themselves out. What can we do about anything? Nothing! Everything is already all right.

Mind Your Business!

No matter how hard I try to keep my thoughts wholesome, my mind will always revert to matters I can't control. I've learned the process of taking mental retreats, which helps release the ever-occurring meaningless thoughts. Nothing is worth taking you to a place of discontent. Usually, those places of discontent aren't even reality. We create worlds in our minds and our minds react to them--what a waste of valuable time.

Stop it! Just stop it and control those thoughts by whatever means necessary. Just as easy as it is to think negative thoughts, it's easy to think wholesome thoughts, but we have to program our minds to do this.

When my younger sister celebrated her 39th birthday, her gift to herself was to fast for the day and give her body the beginning of a cleansing process for her mind, her body, and her soul. I asked her what brought her to this point to make such a decision and she said she wasted every year of her thirties making wrong decisions and was tired of it. She reached the point where she couldn't take it anymore and was tired of battling the same things year after year.

When you reach a point where you are ready to make a change in your life, you'll do it. Nothing anyone says, nothing you read or see will begin the change in you--you are the beginning of change. You have to make the choice to turn away from old ways and habits.

Our environment plays a great part in our thought process. What we watch on television, what we listen to on the radio, what we read, and who we talk to all have a part in our thought process. Trash in--trash out. Guard your mind and program it to reject being succumbed to trash. You may have to stop hanging with certain people--or family. You may have to stop watching particular television shows--we know which ones. Love yourself enough to place yourself in the best environment possible for you and your family. If your husband is the problem, it's time to retreat--in your mind. Don't entertain empty thoughts, get rid of them and focus on you!

The mind is a powerful thing. When we become knowledgeable of that power, our days of peace will be continual. We can't always jump up and leave for the weekend or attend a retreat; however, a retreat is always available within us--in our mind. You may not have the finances to get away, and there are many single mothers who just can't make it happen. We have to get to the point where even in the midst of dirty dishes, a crying baby, a demanding husband, disobedient children, or our own unhappiness, we can retreat in our mind and focus on things more pleasant.

Just as I find peace in the midst of a dirty kitchen, you too can retreat and find peace in your home. The mind is more powerful than we give it credit for. We often focus on what we're doing, which is extremely important, yet we don't have to feed the task. Let me explain.

Cooking isn't one of my favorite things to do, and I have to pray for the desire to walk into the kitchen to prepare meals for my family. When dinner time arrives, I have two choices--I can either whine and complain the whole time I'm cutting, stirring, shaking, and baking or I can accept and acknowledge what needs to be done, just do it, and move on mentally. Attitude is everything.

Here is another example we're all familiar with. How often do you play taxi driver in your home? If you have school-aged children, quite often, I'm sure. Instead of focusing on the trip and the lack of desire to drive back and forth, we can train our mind to visit positive places. Instead of sitting at a stoplight complaining about how long the light is and where you have to be, use the time to pray or meditate. You'll be surprised how quickly the light changes.

As a substitute to a private *why me* party, practice taking some deep breaths and exhaling your negative thoughts out of your system. Whatever works! Concentrated breathing is a no-fail relaxer. We have plenty of time to pour into ourselves, yet we use our valuable time focusing on matters we can't control - such as other people's decisions and actions. I frequently go to paradise while washing the dishes. I even walk along the beach while vacuuming. I don't know where I am when I'm cleaning toilets, but I'm not in that bathroom! Doing this for just one minute makes such a difference in our mindset. Not only are we strengthening ourselves, our family benefits also.

Practicing this a few times a day will create a habit. This habit then conditions us to automatically revert to a place of peace when we feel a snap scenario surfacing. Yes, it takes practice--a great deal of practice, but it's worth it. Your family will appreciate it and so will your mind and body! If you think it's not possible because of your strong personality, short temper, or maybe a generational curse of anger, take it from me. I have all those things, but God is able to work through any mess. If He can do it for me, He can do it for you. Choose to believe the positive, not the negative.

Insignificant mess steals our peace. Entertaining these messy thoughts has the capability of making us feel twisted and angry. We have to learn to control them before they control us

Rest!

There is usually one ingredient in a recipe that tops the taste. Some cooks and bakers like to keep that one ingredient a secret. The secret ingredient to our recipe is REST. Getting the proper rest is key to our peace of mind.

"I'm tired!" Tired should be a woman's middle name. No wonder we snap! When I'm tired, I can't think straight, I'm short with my children, I'm irritable, yet I still go on. I have been so tired, I've felt like walking away from life--now, this is tired! We don't always accurately judge when we need to stop and rest. We think we're doing something great by completing our "to do" list yet we're only hurting ourselves by pushing past our limit. It makes no sense at all for a body to feel the way a tired woman's body does day after day.

My mother used to tell me to close my eyes for a few minutes during the day. She sounded like she was speaking a foreign language to me. "Close my eyes? When?" I could come up with every excuse not to close my eyes or take a power nap. Who has time to take a nap when the house needs cleaning and nobody wants to clean? Who can nap when the family wants to eat and nobody wants to cook? Who can close their eyes when clothes need washing and everyone looks at mama? A nap? Are you kidding me? What about the mothers with infants? They suffer from sleep deprivation and can't recognize the word "nap" much less take one! They rarely sleep, so when does a nap fit in?

Well, I may not take a nap, but I sure have learned to put my feet up and sit on my behind when I need to. I wasn't receiving any "Most Hours Put In" award, so why not stop and relax? Everybody else in the house knows how to put their feet up, so why not the woman of the house? Where's the ottoman? Usually, as soon as I stop to rest, the nap automatically happens anyway. Resting is not only a physical benefit, it's mental also. Your body may be resting although your mind may be working overtime. Our mental ability and capacity is exhibited by the amount of rest we give our bodies and our brain. No wonder we snap--many of us are *always* tired.

Why do we feel guilty when it's time to do something for ourselves? If you've passed this stage, congratulations, nevertheless, there are more mothers feeling guilty than aren't. We've been programmed to think it's selfish to consider ourselves first, when in actuality it's selfish NOT to take care of ourselves first.

I graduated from the stage of feeling guilty a couple of years ago while on a trip to New Orleans with my older sister. As we began our drive, a deep feeling of emptiness came over me. I realized it was because I didn't have my children with me and I usually do--they are my shadows. My sister said I needed to get away more often, which was the truth, but first I needed to get over this dreadful feeling. Well, the further we drove, the better I felt and before we hit the Louisiana state line, I was okay! The three days away cleaned out my mental and emotional pipelines. I felt like a different person. It's hard to describe exactly how I felt, but it felt good--refreshing if you will. There was no one to care for except me. This trip reminded me of how good I *can* feel. I realized it's more selfish to *not* take a break because it denies me and my family of the person I really am. After a woman is refreshed and renewed, she is a different person. If you are tired of looking at your home, your husband, children, co-workers, your neighbors, and maybe even yourself, it's time for a break. If you can't get away, go into another room or take a walk outside. It's time to retreat--you need to rest.

Many women live without a life outside of the family, which can be dangerous. If everything we do is centered around our husband and children, it's time to find an outlet, a hobby, or a friend to occupy some of your time--not all your time, some of your time. I enjoy reading and writing, and I usually stay up late or rise early to do this. I understand it's difficult to find time for ourselves, but nothing is more important than investing in ourselves. I use to require a clean house before I could relax. Even if Sugar Bear wanted me to watch a movie with him, I needed to fold that last load of laundry or make sure the kitchen was clean before I sat down. Now? I realize those dishes will be there when the movie is over and those clothes sure won't fold themselves. They will be there, so I've learned to take a minute for myself.

I encourage you to take a minute for you. There is always a reason to *not* find time for ourselves--it seems like time is against us. No matter what time of day we set aside for ourselves, something comes up. The phone will ring, the baby will cry, the dog will bark, the neighbor will visit, or some other usual happening will attempt to get in our way. What's the solution? Make yourself a priority! If you love yourself, you'll do this.

I used to think my family didn't want me to have time to myself. It seemed like a conspiracy against me! Do they want me burned out and dragging? Do they hate to see me put my feet up? It appears mothers aren't allowed to get physically tired. We need permission to get tired of cooking and cleaning and playing taxi driver. We're supposed to love our job, so to say we need a break may be taken personally. Verbalizing needing a break may suggest we don't enjoy taking care of them. Our cries for help are usually subtle and passively requested until we snap--and then it's not in silence.

Mothers don't desire and require breaks solely for selfish reasons. It's a necessity! Most jobs in America get a break--more than one for an eight hour work day. Why wouldn't a woman need a break as she works non-stop to care for her family?

It makes no sense to me to even think we wouldn't need a break. The butcher, the baker, the candlestick maker, the taxicab driver, the mediator, and the caretaker. These jobs all fall under the title of "Mother"--the most demanding and underrated position in America. The job description of a mother reminds me of my job as an Air Traffic Controller while I served in the Navy. As a controller, my job was to control several airborne airplanes and keep them separated. As a mother, I'm wearing several hats and juggling several balls and can't afford to let any of them fall; each job description is equally important. I could always ask for relief as a controller, yet a mother goes on, and on, and on, and on, and her only relief is when she stops to rest or the children get old enough to share in the workload. When we do rest, no one takes over--the tasks will remain and we pick up where we left off. No offense to my fellow controllers, however, I find it far more difficult being a mother. Both jobs have lives at stake, yet a controller is only authorized to work a specified number of hours per shift, whereas, a mother's job never ends. When I finally acquired the skills to become a good controller, one of my co-workers called me a "cool cucumber." It didn't matter how many airplanes were under my control, my demeanor didn't change. There are skills to keep mothers cool cucumbers also.

Nobody seems to get it. Mothers are burning the candle at both ends and stressed from all angles. We can hardly help ourselves, yet we are called to be helpmates to our husbands. Our families will exhaust us of every ounce of energy we have--if we allow them to. Instead of receiving the needed understanding and compassion mothers cry out for, bystanders continue to ask, request, and yearn for our limited time and energy. We even ask favors of each other as we professionally wear our game faces. What makes us think another woman has time or energy to relieve us of things on our full plate? Isn't her plate just as full?

No wonder our family doesn't understand what we go through--*we* don't understand what we go through! It's admirable to rescue each other when we need assistance, just don't forget to take care of YOU. We all need a break every now and then, though we don't always know *how* to break. Recognizing our breaking point is the key. Knowing our limitations and when to stop is crucial. Not knowing our limits causes irritability and frustration with our family, our marriage, and ourselves. Because we play the game, there is no outlet--no place to go without being criticized or judged, therefore, we snap in silence. This sudden act of snapping can be mentally, physically, or emotionally to ourselves, our children, our husbands, or someone outside the home. The word 'snap' may seem like a harsh word, yet it can also be simply defined as a *melting moment.*

The candle burning at both ends doesn't burn forever. These melting moments are experienced by every woman at various degrees. Although the moments are only temporary, they can have life-long, damaging effects. These melting moments can be controlled or even avoided.

Take a Break!

Retiring from the Navy and staying home with my children was a tough transition. I jumped right into mommy mode without taking time out from my twenty-year career. I remember Sugar Bear coming home from work one day and I expressed my need to take a break. My dear husband may not remember this, but he told me I get a break everyday just being home. I knew at this moment, my relationship with God was going to be strengthened in ways I never imagined. My closeness to my Creator was going to reach heights never imagined! Sugar Bear's statement wasn't a lack of compassion, yet confirmed the necessity of this book for not only women, but husbands and children as well. They don't get it.

Women are often hurt by the family's lack of under-standing and compassion, yet they can't be blamed. We have to remind ourselves we were created as extraordinary, intricate beings. Only the One who created us can completely understand and give us what we need, yet we continue to look for our family to understand and appreciate us. The truth is... they don't know how. Thank God for birthdays and Mother's Day; these are days they hone in on and are conditioned to act. Our loved ones can only try to give us what we need, which is why so many women are disappointed on their birthday and Mother's Day.

Even when prompted to show appreciation on special days, they only know to do what they think we want. Our family has only an idea of who they share a home with.

Practice Body Discipline!

You've neglected your body for years with bad choices and lack of exercise and proper nutrition, so now you have a disease or life-threatening health issue. Imagine a doctor saying this to you. Imagine being told you had less than a year to live unless you made some changes in your lifestyle habits. Most of us would immediately make more than a few drastic changes. Why can't we make these lifestyle changes on our own? Since we do everything else for our family, why can't we add one more thing to the list? Why put ourselves at risk for health problems because of our lack of body discipline.

What exactly is body discipline? Body discipline is the attention we give our bodies in regards to diet and exercise. Diet does not mean losing weight, it is simply the food we choose to give our body. This ingredient has a tendency of leaving a bad taste on our palate. It's the one ingredient many of us don't care for.

How much discipline do you have when it comes to what you allow in your body? How much discipline do you have when it comes to giving your body the exercise it needs? The answer to these questions lies in the level of discipline we have in our life. Our discipline carries over to every aspect of our life.

Your body will only take care of you as well as you take care of your body. Maybe we should pretend our bodies belong to someone else since we're so good at taking care of others. I'll make sure my children get an apple a day--I'll wash it, peel it, cut it, slice it, or dice it, but it's effort for me to have this discipline for myself. Why is this? A woman's body is usually close to last on her list of priorities. Oh sure, we'll take care of the external needs--hair and nails. But we fail to realize the inside controls the outside.

Have you ever popped a cookie or a handful of chips in your mouth first thing in the morning? You're rushing because you didn't wake up early enough to pour into yourself, so you need a booster shot of energy to prepare to pour into everyone else. What's quick and easy? Soda? Chocolate? Wrong foods deliver all the wrong moods. How do I know? Because on too many occasions, I have invited the wrong foods in my body for a quick fix. We are the vehicle our family needs to get things done. If we are low on fuel how are we supposed to have the capability to get everyone else to their destination? Mom's taxi has a deeper meaning than we realize. We are literally the vehicle others will use to get them where they need to be--emotionally, physically, and geographically from point A to point B.

The excuses have to stop. The excuses we choose are now at the point of sounding ridiculous. How do I know? Because I've come up with plenty and finally in my forties, I've made a decision to at least attempt to do the right thing and practice some body discipline. Being the founder of an organization for mothers assigns me the obligation to do the right thing. I'm supposed to walk the walk and talk the talk. Ha! God knows I try, but I'll be the first to admit I love my chocolate and I love to bake. The rest is history. I need to do everything in my power to set the example.

Well, I'm an example of one mother being human with a desire to do the right thing. Yes, I do exercise and I do it right in my home with little equipment: I dance. What excuse do I need for shaking my body to a good beat? There isn't a mother on the planet who is physically able that can't get in front of the television or play some music and move--just move! Get your blood flowing through your body while you're able. Not only will you have more energy and endurance, you'll feel great knowing you are doing something good for yourself.

My father is a serious walker. The body discipline he has is remarkable. He is in his early seventies and has had a few hip surgeries, but walks circles around each of his daughters who are mothers with children. We sometimes use our children as an excuse not to exercise, yet our children should be a prime reasons we *should* exercise.

What we allow in our body on a daily basis and how we treat its needs determines our level of energy, tolerance, peace, and patience throughout the day.

Check the Calendar!

Raging hormones can turn a beautiful woman into a hostile witch. In a matter of seconds we can turn from a comforting caretaker into monster mommy. If we aren't aware of our body changes and know when we are experiencing a chemically imbalanced moment, simple situations can take a turn for the worse and before we know it, we are out of control. Diet and exercise are key factors with our hormones. Check your calendar!

The small things we deal with on a daily basis seem to be amplified during these moments. We know these moments are coming, so we should try to prepare for them. Proper rest, exercise, and nutrition can limit some of the many symptoms that accompany our body changes. Remember your PMS!

Symptoms such as irritability, fatigue, paranoia, and crying spells are just a few of the gifts of hormones. When your husband or significant other all of a suddenly appears ugly to you, or you don't feel like caring for your children or playing your part in life--step back and evaluate your body discipline. What did you eat today? When was the last time you exercised? Running behind your children doesn't count.

Remember your attitude and disposition will affect the entire household. Whoever said we only get one good week a month (moody free) might be right. Whether you choose to see a doctor, take a pill, or retreat to renew your mind, a portion of perfect peace is promised to you.

If you are a woman, you experience the horror of hormones in some degree. Whether it be your monthly cycle, peri-menopause, menopause, PMS, pregnancy, post-partum depression, or some other female fun, we share these feelings--it's in the mix.

Stop Fighting Your Life!

Self-encouragement, prayer/meditation, body discipline, and rest: we now have the recipe to living a life with peace. Using it doesn't excuse the challenges and hardships of life, but they sure will be easier to deal with--I'm a witness. We learn very little in good times. The valuable lessons come in the midst of our tears, our pain, and unfavorable conditions. These growing pains seem to last a lifetime, yet we gain a lifetime of strength and character, which is key in becoming a whole woman. Life's challenges, pitfalls, and victories bring maturity and wisdom. You may not understand why your life has gone the way it has or why you are enduring present situations, but there is a tailor-made plan designed exclusively for your life. God created you and knows exactly what ingredients are needed in the mix of your life to mold you into the woman He created you to be. Stop fighting your life! Encourage yourself. Practice body discipline. Pray or meditate more. Get some rest!

Becoming a woman is a long process; just because our monthly cycle makes its debut doesn't make us a woman. Yes, it would be great to learn from watching another woman's pain and suffering, yet if you don't feel the heat, the mix is not as effective. Since we were created *by* God *for* God's purpose, only He knows what is best for us. So many times, we try to run from our life, yet no matter how dark our situation may appear, how steep our mountain may be, or how low our valley is, our pain is meant to empower. We can either make the best of our situation, or do nothing and snap in silence. We become a better woman, wife, and mother when we go through the fire of life.

No matter what your situation is or how dark and low your present valley may seem, it truly is working out a good thing in your life. You are becoming a better woman, a better mother, a better wife.

Maintain Strength in Storms!

Into every life some rain must fall. Life wouldn't be life without raindrops falling from time to time. Some of us are blessed to have just a few drops fall on us while others may get a drizzle, or a light rain. If you're lucky, you've been chosen to endure a few great rain storms. Our struggles and hardships only build character and make us stronger.

My younger sister use to hate to hear me say "It's not about you." She once told me I have to be careful who I say this to because it sounds harsh--as if I have no compassion. Well, regardless of how it sounds, it's true! Nothing we go through, no matter how few or how great the rain drops are... it's not *only* about you. Blessings are compounded and so are the trials of life. Because we are so self-absorbed, we tend to think those storms are a direct reflection on us. We get in our world of doom and despair and shut everyone else out. This is the importance of taking off our mask and allowing others to look into our life and learn from it.

Quit the game of charades long enough to allow another woman to gain strength and see the awesome power of the pain you've gone through. No, we're not supposed to go around airing all our dirty laundry, yet when the time is right--and you know when it is--unmask and speak up! What right do we have to keep God's gift of healing from another woman? This selfishness only weakens our bond. There are bits and pieces in our life that should be shared with other women going through or about to embark on a journey you're on or you've already completed. Because of the charades game, we keep these embarrassing, yet valuable issues to ourselves. We keep them locked away in our broken hearts.

Share your umbrella as you shelter yourself from the storms of life. What is embarrassing to you may be empowering to another.

Now What?

Now that the secret is out and we know why we snap and how to prevent it, what is the next step? How do we begin to apply what we've read and not allow this to be just another inspiring book for our bookshelf? The bottom line is you'll only make a change when you're ready to genuinely value and love yourself. Loving yourself will allow you to put your needs first and putting your needs first will make for a more peaceful, joyful woman, wife, and mother. Even today I still fall short with my PMS checklist, yet my reprogrammed brain redirects me to immediately get on the right track. No more weeks of missed exercise. No more cookies or cake for a booster breakfast. No more working until my legs hurt. No more getting so hungry I'm mean and irritable. NO MORE! As one songstress wrote, "I love me better than that."

I was a Mother for eleven years before I got to this point, so please don't think it'll happen overnight. It's a process and it takes much body discipline and determination. That determination will flow out of your newfound love for yourself.

Don't start tomorrow--start right now. The ball is in your court. It's up to you. Will you continue to be another tired, frustrated, dissatisfied woman, or will you choose to tackle life and live it to the fullest--with perfect peace--by being whole and happy? Face your limitations and acknowledge your strengths. Encourage yourself and stop waiting on others to encourage you. Get some rest; refresh and renew your mind. Develop some body discipline and allow your character to be strengthened by some re-programming of your thoughts, your reactions, and your love for yourself.

Will you slip up from time to time and forget to practice PMS? Of course you will! While writing this book, I had a night where my PMS checklist was completely absent. I let myself get too far and had a melting moment. What happened? I allowed busyness to blind me of my needs. The boys had soccer practice and it was late when we returned home. They were hungry and so was I because I didn't eat properly before going to practice. I was exhausted because the parents scrimmaged against the children and I forgot how old I was. As I walked into the house, I immediately began unfinished laundry. My bed was already full of clothes and I piled more onto the pile. I attempted to fold them and succeeded after I took a short nap on top of them. My husband was conveniently at school and I didn't have another ounce of energy to be cordial to the boys, so I stayed in my bedroom while they tackled their nighttime regimen on their own including finding something to eat. They know when mama has reached her limit because I disappear without saying a word to anyone. This is a risky state of mind to be in, yet I allowed myself to go there. When my husband finally came home, the boys were ready for bed and said goodnight.

Finally, they were going to sleep. Now I could spend some time with my husband. I was smart enough to have his dinner in the refrigerator, so he helped himself and we sat and talked for a while. The night finally came to a close and as everyone slept peacefully, I was awake typing away at the computer--exhausted. Does this mean my proven plan for perfect peace has holes in it? No, it simply means I did not follow the plan--I'm not perfect!

The PMS checklist will work only if we make it a lifestyle habit. We have to PREVENT getting to the point of snapping. If eating right, exercising, and resting become a part of our existence, we won't meet our breaking point as often as we do. I knew what I needed to do to redirect my path and I did. I fixed myself a snack and put my feet up while enjoying the quietness of my home--in peace.

The Essence Of My Peace

Several months after I thought this book was finished, I received a turbulent test of my peace. A test to offer a life-long passion to share not only peace, but the power of sweet perfect peace with women. Unbeknownst to me, it wasn't *just* a test, it was the final chapter of this book. It confirmed and affirmed what the essence of perfect peace was and is to me.

I've been baking a cake for a couple of years and my husband convinced me to try to market it. He may have forgotten his overzealous act of persuasion; nevertheless, we both agreed to move forward with our popular cake. Sugar Bear has always supported me in all my endeavors and this one was no exception. The week I chose to publicly market the cake was a week my faith, patience, confidence, abilities, and strength as a woman, wife, and mother were tested. I remember it like it was yesterday. It's funny how God will throw things in the mix of our life right before He blesses us. Is He testing our faithfulness or is He testing us to see if we can handle the blessings? Well, I won't try to figure God out, but I know I went through the fire!

I realized just how much Sugar Bear's support and strength meant to me through this test. I needed him like I needed air, although in one of the most important weeks of my life, I found myself gasping for that pillar of air.

At the time, my husband and I were leading the Couples Ministry at our church, so to be under attack wasn't foreign ground to us--it was expected. I was sick and tired of my marriage going through storms and can't even remember what this storm was about, but I *did* remember I was about to embark upon a blessing that would change my family's life. This storm was necessary to become who I am today. God was preparing me and also giving me the final chapter of this book.

The day our baking business was making its big premiere, not only was my husband missing in action, but my younger sister and mother were literally missing in action. They had a ninety-minute drive to get to me, but because they took a wrong turn, they were delayed. I need to mention they travel Hwy 65 each time they visit me, so why did they have to miss their exit on this very important day? Well, their absence was just an additional ingredient in my mix on this ultimate test of my peace.

My children weren't excluded from this mix either. Since they have my undivided attention everyday, they wondered why this day wasn't about them. Yes, I dared to do something outside of being mama. They continually got in my way as I scrambled to get everything together. When I arrived at the location of the premiere, the door was locked. The owner left because I was late, so I sat in my car to catch my breath and refocus. While sitting there, I noticed my decorator was also missing in action. Good grief. Lord, why today? Where is my help? Is there anything else You want to throw in my mix?

At this point, I was mentally exhausted and I was about to snap! I sat in my car questioning God while at the same time praying for His mercy and peace. The day seemed surreal. "Is this really happening to me--today?

Lord, you must really love me to take me through this--today!" Minutes later, a car drove up and parked next to mine. It was a friend arriving to see if I needed help. I got out of my car, got on my knees, looked up and yelled, "Thank you, Jesus!" The

Lord had removed all my help only to remind me to keep my mind on Him. Ahhh… my source of perfect peace: the Prince of Peace!

Needless to say, more help arrived and things began to fall in place for the cake premiere. Although we were late getting started, the premiere was a big success. The day didn't go as I planned, but because I did my best to go with the flow, it was better than I expected it to be. I didn't cry or yell at anyone and I kept my peace of mind. I didn't snap, but there were a few melting moments that surely could have led to it. God knew exactly what mix I needed this particular day. He even sent reinforcements throughout the day of the premiere to remind me everything was alright--as long as I kept my mind on Him. I could have tried to fix things and manipulate what God already put in place, yet I remained as calm as I possibly could, prayed, and went with the flow of things, as messed up as they appeared to my carnal eyes.

The dark side of me wanted to curse my husband, lock my children up in a room, fire my volunteer help, and cancel the premiere. I couldn't believe what was happening to me, but I had to remember all the good advice I give others.

"It's not about you."

"It's already alright."

"It is what it is."

I had to talk myself to higher ground--a place of peace. Ladies, perfect peace is real. I *know* perfect peace.

Before I could share this book or speak peace with anyone, I had to be sure I knew peace for myself. Not my mother's peace. Not my grandmother's peace. Not my pastor's peace, but my own peace.

I passed my test. Sugar Bear and the boys survived not being number one for a day. I matured as a woman and my belief in God's promise of perfect peace went to another level. Did the test hurt? Yes! Did I wonder if I would make it through the storm? Yes! Did I come out of the storm stronger and wiser?

Yes! No matter what we go through or how dark our skies may be--we are promised perfect peace in the midst of it.

By the way, we named the cake Perfect Peace and it symbolizes everything thrown in the mix of my life and how it all makes sense if I follow God's recipe. Now that I know, that I know, that I know the true power of peace, I'm passing the peace to you! May peace be unto you.

Appendix: PMS (Preventive Maintenance of Self) Checklist

Get started with your PMS checklist today! Getting it on paper will help you realize the areas you need improvement on. Don't neglect yourself; nurture your *self*. Take note of your daily PMS.

Keeping track of your *self* will help you better understand your *self*. Develop a habit of *self* inventory. After a while, it'll be an automatic mental reminder to take care of YOU.

Preventative Maintenance of Self Questions	M	T	W	TH	F	SA	SU
Have I encouraged myself?							
Have I prayed or meditated?							
Have I reacted in peace?							
Have I minded my business?							
Have I rested?							

Have I taken a break?							
Have I practiced body discipline by exercising?							
Have I checked the calendar?							
Have I stopped fighting my life?							
Have I maintained strength in storms?							

NOTES:

Appendix: PMS (Preventive Maintenance of Self) Checklist

Get started with your PMS checklist today! Getting it on paper will help you realize the areas you need improvement on. Don't neglect yourself; nurture your *self*. Take note of your daily PMS.

Keeping track of your *self* will help you better understand your *self*. Develop a habit of *self* inventory. After a while, it'll be an automatic mental reminder to take care of YOU.

Preventative Maintenance of Self Questions	M	T	W	TH	F	SA	SU
Have I encouraged myself?							
Have I prayed or meditated?							
Have I reacted in peace?							
Have I minded my business?							
Have I rested?							
Have I taken a break?							

Have I practiced body discipline by exercising?							
Have I checked the calendar?							
Have I stopped fighting my life?							
Have I maintained strength in storms?							

NOTES:

Appendix: PMS (Preventive Maintenance of Self) Checklist

Get started with your PMS checklist today! Getting it on paper will help you realize the areas you need improvement on. Don't neglect yourself; nurture your *self*. Take note of your daily PMS.

Keeping track of your *self* will help you better understand your *self*. Develop a habit of *self* inventory. After a while, it'll be an automatic mental reminder to take care of YOU.

Preventative Maintenance of Self Questions	M	T	W	TH	F	SA	SU
Have I encouraged myself?							
Have I prayed or meditated?							
Have I reacted in peace?							
Have I minded my business?							
Have I rested?							
Have I taken a break?							

Have I practiced body discipline by exercising?							
Have I checked the calendar?							
Have I stopped fighting my life?							
Have I maintained strength in storms?							

NOTES:

Appendix: PMS (Preventive Maintenance of Self) Checklist

Get started with your PMS checklist today! Getting it on paper will help you realize the areas you need improvement on. Don't neglect yourself; nurture your *self*. Take note of your daily PMS.

Keeping track of your *self* will help you better understand your *self*. Develop a habit of *self* inventory. After a while, it'll be an automatic mental reminder to take care of YOU.

Preventative Maintenance of Self Questions	M	T	W	TH	F	SA	SU
Have I encouraged myself?							
Have I prayed or meditated?							
Have I reacted in peace?							
Have I minded my business?							
Have I rested?							
Have I taken a break?							

Have I practiced body discipline by exercising?							
Have I checked the calendar?							
Have I stopped fighting my life?							
Have I maintained strength in storms?							

NOTES:

Appendix: PMS (Preventive Maintenance of Self) Checklist

Get started with your PMS checklist today! Getting it on paper will help you realize the areas you need improvement on. Don't neglect yourself; nurture your *self*. Take note of your daily PMS.

Keeping track of your *self* will help you better understand your *self*. Develop a habit of *self* inventory. After a while, it'll be an automatic mental reminder to take care of YOU.

Preventative Maintenance of Self Questions	M	T	W	TH	F	SA	SU
Have I encouraged myself?							
Have I prayed or meditated?							
Have I reacted in peace?							
Have I minded my business?							
Have I rested?							
Have I taken a break?							

Have I practiced body discipline by exercising?							
Have I checked the calendar?							
Have I stopped fighting my life?							
Have I maintained strength in storms?							

NOTES:

Appendix: PMS (Preventive Maintenance of Self) Checklist

Get started with your PMS checklist today! Getting it on paper will help you realize the areas you need improvement on. Don't neglect yourself; nurture your *self*. Take note of your daily PMS.

Keeping track of your *self* will help you better understand your *self*. Develop a habit of *self* inventory. After a while, it'll be an automatic mental reminder to take care of YOU.

Preventative Maintenance of Self Questions	M	T	W	TH	F	SA	SU
Have I encouraged myself?							
Have I prayed or meditated?							
Have I reacted in peace?							
Have I minded my business?							
Have I rested?							
Have I taken a break?							

Have I practiced body discipline by exercising?							
Have I checked the calendar?							
Have I stopped fighting my life?							
Have I maintained strength in storms?							

NOTES:

Appendix: PMS (Preventive Maintenance of Self) Checklist

Get started with your PMS checklist today! Getting it on paper will help you realize the areas you need improvement on. Don't neglect yourself; nurture your *self*. Take note of your daily PMS.

Keeping track of your *self* will help you better understand your *self*. Develop a habit of *self* inventory. After a while, it'll be an automatic mental reminder to take care of YOU.

Preventative Maintenance of Self Questions	M	T	W	TH	F	SA	SU
Have I encouraged myself?							
Have I prayed or meditated?							
Have I reacted in peace?							
Have I minded my business?							
Have I rested?							
Have I taken a break?							

Have I practiced body discipline by exercising?							
Have I checked the calendar?							
Have I stopped fighting my life?							
Have I maintained strength in storms?							

NOTES: